Someone knows everything about you—EVERY-THING! He knows what you think and what you plan to say before you even open your mouth. Your triumphs and victories, your heartaches and failures are no mystery to Him.

God knows. He knows you upside down and inside out. And He still loves you. Just as a loving father loves his children.

But do you know God? Do you have an intimate, close relationship with Him? You can. *You and God: The Abba Relationship* can help you. Learn to relate to God in a new way—as your Abba.

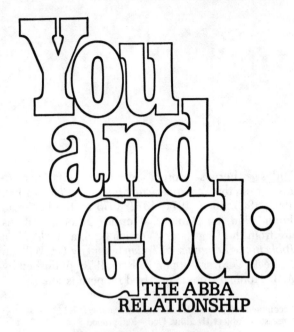

You and God:

THE ABBA RELATIONSHIP

Dr. Timothy Foster

While this book is designed for the reader's personal enjoyment and profit, it is also intended for group study. A Leader's Guide with Multiuse Transparency Masters is available from your local bookstore or from the publisher at $2.95.

VICTOR BOOKS

a division of SP Publications, Inc.

WHEATON, ILLINOIS 60187

Offices also in Fullerton, California • Whitby, Ontario, Canada • Amersham-on-the-Hill, Bucks, England

Recommended Dewey Decimal Classification: 231.1
Suggested Subject Heading: God—Fatherhood

Library of Congress Catalog Card Number: 80-50856
ISBN: 0-88207-221-8

VICTOR BOOKS
A division of SP Publications, Inc.
P.O. Box 1825 • Wheaton, Illinois 60187

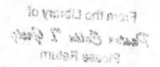

CONTENTS

This book is dedicated to my loving wife
Donna
and our daughters Tanya and Tara.
Without these three, I would never
have known about "daddyhood."

PREFACE

Having a book published is, for me, like giving birth—a mixture of joy and pain. I admit I've never given birth, nor am I the least bit disappointed that husbands and fathers are denied that "privilege." But each time something I've written is released to the public, I find myself fearful of being misunderstood, or worse yet, understood and disagreed with.

With this book, I've had enough reaction ahead of time that I think I can predict what most of the complaints will be: "Too familiar with God." "Not enough respect for God's majesty." "Not enough regard for God's holiness."

I agree that we need to see God as majestic, powerful, and awesome. We need to know more and more about who God is in all of His various aspects and facets.

This little book is *not* intended to be an exhaustive study of God. It's not called *All About God*. Rather, this book takes a look at *one* of the names of God; it examines only one of the ways in which God has chosen to reveal Himself to us.

Don't let this one attribute be all you know about God. Study all of Him that you can. I am trying to do that. In fact, it was out of a bigger plan of trying to know God that this book came to be.

AUTHOR'S NOTE

And God said to Moses, "I AM WHO I AM"; and He said, "Thus you shall say to the sons of Israel, 'I AM has sent me to you.' "

Exodus 3:14

1
THE NAMES OF GOD

Years ago God began to teach me some startling, yet exciting lessons about Himself. My daughter Tanya was sitting in her high chair and I was feeding her. She had just finished her required half jar of strained carrots and it was time for the half jar of applesauce. But there was a problem. Tanya had her two little hands around the jar of carrots and she wouldn't let go.

I tried vainly to explain that it was time for the applesauce but she wasn't interested or even tuned in to what I wanted. I could have just ripped the jar out of her hands, but I didn't want to treat her that way. Finally in desperation I said to her, "Just trust me. I have something better for you. Let go of that nasty old stuff. Just trust me."

At that instant, God spoke to me in a voice so clear that it was almost audible. "Yes," He said, "that's just what you do to Me. You keep holding on to what you have, and you won't let go even though I have something better for you. Trust Me, just trust Me."

Since then I've been paying more attention to the fact that God calls Himself our Father. This book deals with that very special fact about God, and the implications of God's fatherliness.

I believe the impact of "God is our Father" will be greater if we take time to see how God revealed His offer to be our Father.

Progressive Revelation

When little children first begin to ask, "Where did I come from?" wise parents give answers which are truthful, but limited to the level of understanding of their children. This means, of course, that the first several answers to the question are incomplete.

As a professional psychologist, I have counseled several patients of both sexes who were confused and damaged by learning too much too soon about the mysteries of conception and birth. They learned more than they were prepared to understand.

In a similar way, God knew it was necessary to reveal Himself to His children in progressive steps, rather than all at once. In this way it was easier for His children to learn and respond to Him, a little at a time. One way to trace the progress of this revelation is to study the names of God.

Old Testament Names of God

One of the earliest names of God used was the name *Elohim*. This word apparently came from a root which meant "to be smitten with fear." *Elohim* is a plural form and may have been related to some form of primitive ancestor worship. This name pictures God as very strong and as the object of fear.

When Tara, my youngest daughter, first went to nursery school, that school and that teacher meant nothing to her. She only knew that she was being removed from the security of her home. She was afraid. Later, as she learned more about school, her response changed.

In a similar way, as man's knowledge and experience with God increased, God introduced a new name for Himself. This new name, *Adonai*, meant "to judge or rule." In other words the first followers of God were spiritually enlightened so that they also saw God as a Judge or Ruler. This name implied that man was the servant of God. Obviously, being God's servant was more fulfilling than relating to God as the "feared One."

Yet God revealed still more of Himself. Next He disclosed Himself as the God of all power who would subject all things to His work of grace and comfort. The name was *El Shaddai* and it was with this name that He identified Himself to Abraham (Gen. 17:1).

We can already see differences between God's earliest name of fear and His later name of comfort. Of course, it is important to point out that later knowledge does not do away with earlier knowledge. Rather, it is simply additional knowledge.

These earliest names were gradually replaced by the name *Yahweh*. *Jehovah*, a more common pronunciation of *Yahweh*, dates from A.D. 1518. *Yahweh* was such a sacred name that the Jews would not pronounce it. They claimed this was in keeping with the third commandment of the Mosaic Law. When reading, they substituted the name *Adonai* for *Yahweh*. The vowels of *Adonai* were added to the consonants "J h w h" to form the name *Jehovah*.

In Exodus 3:14, *Yahweh* is translated "I am that I am." Specifically, this name seems to refer to the fact that God never changes in His relationship with His people. It stresses His faithfulness: "I will be to you what I was to your fathers."

It is difficult for us to grasp the full meaning of this concept that God never changes. I honestly admit that I haven't been aware enough of it myself.

But rather than focus on guilt at this point, let's

remember that God loves us anyway. God's affection and goals for us do not change with our ups and downs, or our successes and failures. No matter how much we change, God is always the same (Mal. 3:6).

For years, scientists have known that they could produce neuroses in laboratory animals by treating those animals in such a way that they never knew what to expect. In my own practice, I've counseled with many people who can trace their neuroses back to their childhood years. As children, they never knew what to expect from their parents. They never knew whether they would be hugged, beaten, or ignored.

Most of us have seen a frightened puppy who has been tormented by selfish children. These youngsters never treated the dog the same way twice. God is not pleased when we relate to Him like a scared puppy, so He revealed more of Himself than just His being the object of fear. He showed that He never changes.

New Testament Names of God

There are basically three names for God recorded in the New Testament. The word *Theos* was used most commonly to mean God, and was used to refer to heathen gods as well. It can be a common noun (he is a god), or a proper noun (You are God).

The word *kurios* refers to the one with power

and authority. It is usually translated "Lord," and refers not only to God, but also to Jesus.

Finally, we come to the last name used for God and that is *pater*, the word translated "father." This name refers to God's relationship with Israel. It designates God as the Source or the Creator and as the Father of all believers. It also refers to the relationship between the Father and the Son.

By studying God's names, we can better understand what He is really like. As we learn more about Him, we can develop a stronger relationship with Him.

And He said to me, "Your son Solomon is the one who shall build My house and My courts; for I have chosen him to be a son to Me, and I will be a Father to him."

1 Chronicles 28:6

2
GOD IS
OUR FATHER

God's offer of Fatherhood, through belief in His Son, is one of the most basic and fundamental truths of theology. We cannot know God without accepting His Fatherhood. And, of course, this book is built upon that premise.

In unconditional love, God has chosen to present Himself to us as our Father. He calls us and indeed makes us His children if we accept His offer of adoption into His family through His Son Jesus.

Why use an entire chapter to prove that God wants us to see Him as our Father—something that most readers probably already accept anyway?

The answer is that some ideas that we accept as

presuppositions may not be true at all. And our other presuppositions may be points of theology built on a flimsy foundation. But the fact that God wants us to see Him as our Father is presented with overwhelming clarity in God's Word.

Old Testament—Father to Israel

As we turn to God's Word to see how He began to reveal Himself as Father, we see the first instance of this when God talked to Moses.

> And the Lord said to Moses, "When you go back to Egypt . . . then you shall say to Pharaoh, 'Thus says the Lord, "Israel is My son, My firstborn." So I said to you, "Let My son go, that he may serve Me"; but you refused to let him go. Behold, I will kill your son, your firstborn" ' " (Ex. 4:21–23).

When God announced Israel was His son, He came to Israel's defense. In essence, the Lord's message to Pharaoh was something like this: "Hey, that's My son! You can't treat him that way. I won't allow it!"

That makes me smile deep inside. Here's the way we would have said it back in suburban Philadelphia: "My dad stuck up for me."

As a practicing psychologist, I talk with a lot of hurting people. Again and again, I realize how many of those hurts could have been avoided if a dad or mom would have stood up, spoken up, and stuck up for his or her own child.

Most emotional damage to children is done by one parent, with the other parent sitting quietly by. The silent parent, the one who says nothing, often thinks that he is keeping the peace. I'm sure that some readers even now feel enraged at a parent who failed to protect them when they were growing up.

I'll say it again. We see from this passage that when God claimed Israel as His son, He went immediately to Israel's defense.

Why did God wait until the Israelite nation was in bondage in Egypt before making this Father-son announcement? The answer is obvious. When the Jews went to Egypt, they were not yet a nation. They were only an extended family.

You will remember that the brothers of Joseph decided to move their families to Egypt. It was in Egypt that the descendants of Abraham, Isaac, and Jacob grew from a family to a nation. God had promised to bless Abraham. By calling Abraham's descendants His own sons, God began to fulfill that promise of blessing.

God's Choice

Before moving on to the next passage, we should notice one important fact. When God talked to Moses, an Israelite, He did not tell Moses to announce His Fatherhood to all the Jews. God, through Moses, was announcing His special relationship with Israel to Pharaoh by saying, "Let My son go."

Why didn't God make some formal announcement to the Israelites about His adopting them, before He announced it to Pharaoh? The answer is twofold. First, God was fulfilling a covenant with Abraham (long dead by this time). God had already had a formal ceremony with Abraham to note that covenant (Gen. 15:5–21).

Second, God was clearly the Initiator in the Father-son relationship. The Israelites did not band together and ask to be made God's sons. God did the choosing. It reminds us that before we ever existed, God knew us and loved us.

This choosing of Israel in its youth is also referred to in Hosea. "When Israel was a youth I loved him, and out of Egypt I called My son" (Hosea 11:1). God did not wait until the Israelites became great to choose them—as a result of their own greatness. Rather, God loved Israel in the nation's youth, while the people were still slaves.

This is a consistent trait of God's character. He often sets things up to demonstrate that He is the Source and not we ourselves. His actions toward us are not dependent on our successes or our works. However, God's unconditional love is so alien to us that we often act as though God won't love us if we're not good.

One of the most frequent responses to God's plan of salvation is that people say, "We're not good enough." Of course we're not. That's why we need saving. God deserves and demands the glory for being the Initiator, the Energizer, and the Sealer of our salvation.

This idea is illustrated by the fact that God chose to adopt Israel when it was a baby nation, and before Israel was even aware of what was happening. It is a lot like adopting a baby at birth. The adoptive parents initiate the action because they want to share their love. The baby naturally responds to the love that is offered.

In those days of ancient Egypt there were two kinds of sons: the firstborn, who was the heir of the father, and all the others. This situation could be compared to that of the royal family in England. The Queen's children fall into two categories—the crown prince, and everyone else.

In this Exodus 4 passage, God called Israel not only His son, but His firstborn. This was why all the firstborn offspring in Egypt were killed, because Pharaoh was severely persecuting God's firstborn. "Israel is My firstborn, and you are refusing to let him go. I will therefore kill your firstborn."

God could have killed off all the slaves, servants, or pets—if that would have represented how He felt about His people. But He didn't. "Now it came about at midnight that the Lord struck all the firstborn in the land of Egypt, from the firstborn of Pharaoh who sat on his throne to the firstborn of the captive who was in the dungeon, and all the firstborn of cattle . . . there was no home where there was not someone dead" (Ex. 12:29–30). The whole Egyptian population was affected by this plague.

The Father of Kings

After the Israelites finished wandering in the wilderness, they established themselves as a nation. Because of their desire to be like other nations, they begged God to give them a king.

Saul, the first king of Israel, was a proud man who disobeyed God. But the second king David was a man after God's own heart. David blessed God and acknowledged Him as the Father of Israel. "So David blessed the Lord in the sight of all the assembly; and David said, 'Blessed art Thou, O Lord God of Israel our Father, forever and ever' " (1 Chron. 29:10).

God reaffirmed His promise of Fatherhood to David's son Solomon. When explaining this, King David said, "And He said to me, 'Your son Solomon is the one who shall build My house and My courts; for I have chosen him to be a son to Me, and I will be a Father to him' " (1 Chron. 28:6).

God sent prophets to repeat His promises to the children of Israel. Isaiah wrote, "Listen, O heavens, and hear, O earth; for the Lord speaks, 'Sons I have reared and brought up, but they have revolted against Me. An ox knows its owner, and a donkey its master's manger, but Israel does not know [its Father], My people do not understand' " (Isa. 1:2–3).

Hosea also wrote about this subject. "Yet the number of the sons of Israel will be like the sand of the sea, which cannot be measured or numbered; and it will come about that, in the place where it is said to them, 'You are not My people,' it will be said to them, 'You are the sons of the living God' " (Hosea 1:10).

Once again, the people of Israel were reminded of God's promises by the Prophet Jeremiah. "Then I said, 'How I would set you among My sons, and give you a pleasant land, the most beautiful inheritance of the nations!' And I said, 'You shall call Me, "My Father," and not turn away from following Me' " (Jer. 3:19).

From these passages in the Old Testament, we see that God chose to adopt the nation of Israel as His son. God reiterated His offer to each generation, from the beginning of the nation of slaves through the kings and prophets. But in spite of God's repeated offer, Israel never responded consistently to God. Sometimes the Israelites responded appropriately and were blessed. Often they rebelled and lost their blessing.

New Testament—Father to All who Accept

As God continued to reveal more about Himself

and His plan for redemption, we see a significant change in His offer of Fatherhood. The Old Testament Jews continued their off-again, on-again Father-child relationship with God, up to the time of Jesus. When Jesus came, He presented *Himself* as the only way to the Father. This offer was first made just to the Jews.

But the Jews were already comfortable with their external veneer of holiness and chose to keep that rather than to become sons of God. In the New Testament, God no longer limited His offer to the nation of Israel.

My Father, Your Father

Jesus often referred to God's offer of Fatherhood. Of course Jesus was very much aware of God (the Father) as His own Father, but He clearly equated that with the Father-child relationship which was offered to all who believe. Jesus said, "See that you do not despise one of these little ones, for I say to you, that their angels in heaven continually behold the face of My Father who is in heaven. . . . Thus it is not the will of your Father who is in heaven that one of these little ones perish" (Matt. 18:10, 14).

For Jesus, "My Father" and "Your Father" meant the same thing. The passages in which Jesus referred to God as our Father are so many that it would be impossible to quote them all. But it is not an exaggeration to say that Jesus referred to Jehovah as "Father" (both His and ours), more than any other name or title.

Here is one brief example of the way Jesus used *Father* in His speech. (The italics are the author's.) "But when you give alms, do not let your left hand know what your right hand is doing that your alms may be in secret; and your *Father* who sees in secret will repay you. . . . But you, when you pray, go into your inner room, and when you have shut your door, pray to your *Father* who is in secret, and your *Father* who sees in secret will repay you. . . . Your *Father* knows what you need, before you ask Him. Pray, then, in this way: 'Our *Father* who art in heaven. . . .' For if you forgive men for their transgressions, your heavenly *Father* will also forgive you" (Matt. 6:3–4, 6, 8–9, 14).

"Father" in the Epistles

Jesus' teaching of God as our Father was continued as a central theme by the apostles. Most of the New Testament epistles were written by the Apostle Paul, and they were written to Christian churches which contained some Jews. But Paul's letters were addressed primarily to Gentile Christians.

Paul's letter to the Romans begins: "Grace to you and peace from God our Father and the Lord Jesus Christ" (Rom. 1:7). Perhaps one such greeting would not be impressive. But similar greetings also appear in eight of Paul's other letters (see 1 Cor. 1:3; Gal. 1:3; Eph. 1:2; Phil. 1:2; Col. 1:2; 1 Thes. 1:1; 2 Thes. 1:2; Titus 1:4).

It is also significant that Paul, under the inspiration of the Holy Spirit, quoted promises originally given to Israel and applied them to Gentile Christians. In 2 Corinthians 6:16–18 Paul wrote, "We are the temple of the living God; just as God said, 'I will dwell in them and walk among them; and I will be their God, and they shall be My people. Therefore, come out from their midst and be separate,' says the Lord. 'And do not touch what is unclean; and I will welcome you. And *I will be a Father to you, and you shall be sons and daughters to Me,*' says the Lord Almighty." (Paul quoted here from Lev. 26:12; Isa. 52:11; and Hosea 1:10.)

As a result of Christ's sacrifice, we have been reconciled to God and "as many as received Him, to them gave He power to become the sons of God" (John 1:12, kjv). God's offer of Fatherhood is now available to all who believe in Jesus.

And finally, Jesus' close friend, the Apostle John wrote, "See how great a love the Father has bestowed on us, that we should be called children of God; and such we are" (1 John 3:1).

The Bible gives ample evidence that God is and wants to be our Father. His plan from the beginning was to make us actively His children. Let's thank the Father for His offer of sonship to us and thank the Son, Jesus, for making our adoption possible.

And because you are sons, God has sent forth the Spirit of His Son into our hearts, crying, "Abba! Father!"
Galatians 4:6

3
THE MEANING
OF ABBA

We have seen how the names people used for God in Scripture reflected their responses to God's continuing revelation of Himself. Each name indicated a more complete understanding of God's nature.

Today, with the complete biblical revelation available to us, we can grasp the scope of God's revelation about Himself. With our full knowledge comes a sense of gratitude. We can be thankful that we live in the age of "the Father God" rather than back in the age of "the feared God."

What's It All About?
When given, the name *Abba* added a new dimension to God's progressive revelation. It conveyed

the idea of a sense of closeness, affection, and confidence which had not been present before.

For believers today, the name *Abba* represents an aspect of our relationship with God that has been overlooked in much of the teaching we have heard about God. Let's examine the actual word *Abba* and its roots.

Most Christians are aware that the original Old Testament was written in the Hebrew language by Moses, David, and a host of others. Of course Hebrew was not written with the Roman alphabet that we use when we write. But if we were to write the Hebrew word for *father* with our own alphabet, we would write it *ab*. This word was used to refer to the male parent. Also, *ab* meant "source" or "inventor," in the same sense that we refer to George Washington as the "father of our country."

While the New Testament was written in a form of Greek, most of the Jews in New Testament times spoke a language related to Hebrew called Aramaic. However, the actual word used for *father* in the New Testament was the Greek word which we would spell *paterno*. *Paterno* is the source of our English word *paternity*, which means "fatherhood."

Jesus' Word for Father

The word *ab* (Hebrew) is used in the Old Testament for father and the word *paterno* (Greek) is used in the New Testament for father with only three exceptions. Those exceptions are the three times when God the Father is called *Abba*. This is the name that Jesus used when He called out to God.

Many readers have probably already noticed the similarity between the Hebrew word for father, *Ab* and Jesus' word, *Abba*. The relationship between the two words is identical to the relationship between the words *dad* and *daddy*.

Picture several young children playing in a park and imagine them calling out to their daddies. You can hear them calling "Papa," "Daddy," "Abba." Yes, the actual word attributed to Jesus in the New Testament as He called out to God was His word for "Daddy."

The first time we find *Abba* used is in Mark 14:36. Let's look at the surrounding verses to understand the circumstances involved in this use of the word:

> And they came to a place called Gethsemane and He said to His disciples, "Sit here until I have prayed." And He took with Him Peter and James and John, and began to be very distressed and troubled. And He said to them, "My soul is deeply grieved to the point of death; remain here and keep watch." And He went a little beyond them, and

fell to the ground, and began to pray
that if it were possible, the hour might
pass Him by. And He was saying,
"Abba! Father! All things are possible
for Thee; remove this cup from Me; yet
not what I will, but what Thou wilt."
And He came and found them sleeping
and said to Peter, "Simon, are you
asleep? Could you not keep watch for
one hour?" (Mark 14:32–37)

Jesus described Himself to His best friends as
"very distressed, troubled, and deeply grieved to
the point of death." These were His closest
friends, the ones with whom He shared His
deepest, most private hurts and fears. But at the
time when Jesus was greatly troubled, they fell
asleep.

Like many of you, I've experienced times in my
life when I too was very distressed and deeply
grieved. At these times I thank God that He has
provided dear friends and family to listen and to
care.

Jesus' pain was worse than mine, yet His
friends failed to act like friends. They had always
been ready when Jesus wanted to give. But when
He needed them, they were emotionally absent.

This left Jesus the Man emotionally needy and
alone, facing physical torture, desertion, be-
trayal, and mockery. He was being rejected by

His followers and by the religious leaders from the entire country where He lived. He was facing certain, slow, and painful death.

Yet worst of all, He knew He would be separated from God. Jesus, the perfect Son of God, was to have placed on Him each sin ever committed by every man, woman, and child who ever had lived or ever would live. Jesus knew that even God would turn away from Him at that time.

Where did He go under anguish like that? Jesus fell down to the ground and cried out to His Abba.

He Is Our Abba Too

It is emotionally moving to see how real was Christ's pain and need. In prayer He called to His only Source of relief, His Abba. But let's resist the temptation to stop here and gaze at the emotional scenery. Let's move on to survey the other two times the name *Abba* appears in the Bible.

This next biblical passage explicitly gives us a new name for God, the name *Abba*.

> But when the fullness of the time came, God sent forth His Son, born of a woman, born under the Law, in order that He might redeem those who were under the Law, that we might receive the adoption as sons. And because you are sons, God has sent forth the Spirit of His Son into our hearts, crying, "Abba!

Father!" Therefore you are no longer a slave, but a son; and if a son, then an heir through God (Gal. 4:4–7).

This passage does not emphasize the fact that Jesus used this name, or that we can use this name if we so desire. Rather, this passage declares that God sent His Spirit to us to make us want to relate to God as *our* Abba.

It is remarkable that Christians have been so slow to respond, so slow to call God *Abba*. Even the translators of the Scriptures from the original languages to our English versions have hesitated. They have usually written "Abba, Father," rather than simply translating the word as it is—the familiar form of "Father."

Note the progression mentioned in this passage. God, through Jesus, bought us out of slavery. But He didn't keep us as slaves or possessions (even though He purchased us). God adopted us into the family and called us *sons*.

I am reminded of a friend who was adopted when he was a young boy of four. His natural father had been a cruel man who had never even cared for his son's most basic needs. But the new mother was warm and loving; the new father obliged his wife because he knew how important the child was to her.

The new father saw to the training of the boy and took care of his physical needs. The boy was well cared for and much better off than before.

But I clearly remember one incident that my friend shared with me. It happened one day when the boy had called his new father, "Daddy." His father stood up straight and said, "I think it would be more manly of you if you would call me 'Father.' "

Isn't that sad? We all need to be loved by and to feel close to our parents. God knows that need very well. It is for this reason that when God adopted us, He did not keep us emotionally isolated from Himself. He offered and still offers His love. Because He desires close fellowship with us, He sent His Spirit to draw us nearer and allow us to call Him *Abba*.

Think of the changes referred to in Galatians 4:7. God has not just adopted us. Through His limitless grace, He has done a much more amazing work. We have been transformed from slaves to sons, and from sons to heirs.

In biblical times, only the first son or the specially chosen son could be the heir. The struggle between Jacob and Esau over the birthright exemplified this fact.

But God has made us more than stepchildren. He has actually shared the inheritance of the Son with us, the former slaves. That inheritance consists of more than financial riches. It can be much better described as personal completeness. God wants to complete our personalities.

Dependable Daddy

I remember a young toddler Trisha whose mother was once my patient. Trisha's dad had died very suddenly. The terrible shock and grief, along with the added financial burden, had caused that young widow to seek counseling.

Trisha had always been a very sensitive and somewhat clingy child. But the loss of her dad, plus her mother having to work and send Trisha to her grandmother's during the day, made little Trisha extremely dependent and timid.

Some time later, Trisha's mother married a young pastor. My wife and I were delighted one day when this family stopped by to see us. I was surprised as well as pleased when Trisha called to her new father, "Catch me, Daddy!" as she jumped out of a tree into his arms. Having a daddy she could count on made a big difference in Trisha's personality.

Often, we must consciously make an effort to realize intellectually and emotionally that God is that kind of dependable Daddy to us. Even though we are grown up, a spiritual relationship like this can give our lives a new dimension.

No Fear

The third passage that uses the word *Abba* is in Romans 8.

For all who are being led by the Spirit of

God, these are sons of God. For you have not received a spirit of slavery leading to fear again, but you have received a spirit of adoption as sons by which we cry out, "Abba! Father!" The Spirit Himself bears witness with our spirit that we are children of God, and if children, heirs also, heirs of God and fellow heirs with Christ (Rom. 8:14–17).

This passage differs from the passage in Galatians on one important point. From these verses in Romans, we see that by no longer being slaves, we no longer need to fear.

It is not at all unusual for me as a psychologist to talk to a person who is incomplete as an adult because of a lack of a daddy when he was a child. Often the daddy left his child when he was divorcing his wife. Sometimes the father didn't even explain to the child what was wrong or why he was leaving. Every child desperately needs to hear his departing father say, "I'll still be your daddy." But some fathers find these words too difficult to express.

The shock of this kind of a loss to a child's, and subsequently, to an adult's personality can leave a lasting scar. It can make a person nervous and frightened all the rest of his life. This fear is referred to here in the Book of Romans.

The lack of fear is linked with crying out "Abba,

Father." "You have not received a spirit of slavery leading to fear again, but you have received a spirit of adoption as sons by which we cry out, 'Abba! Father!' " (v. 15)

Whatever it means to call God *Abba,* it is the opposite of fear. Slavery produces fear. Adoption produces trust. What is the opposite of fear? It is confidence, security, and a sense of everything being under control. Abba is the source of these.

The Fear of the Lord

We have just seen that relating to God as Abba produces the opposite of fear in the lives of God's children. However, the psalmist writes, "The fear of the Lord is the beginning of wisdom" (Ps. 111:10). In the Book of Proverbs we read, "The fear of the Lord is the beginning of knowledge" (Prov. 1:7). We would, therefore, be both foolish (opposite of wisdom) and stupid (opposite of knowledge) if we did not fear God.

What is the difference between the fear of the Lord mentioned in these verses and the fear which Abba removes? Abba removes those feelings that we commonly associate with fear or fright. The other word for fear refers to an appropriate attitude toward God, which includes genuine awe and reverence.

A Word of Caution

Many sincere Christians are upset at the idea of

thinking about Almighty God, our heavenly Father, as our Daddy. I genuinely appreciate their concern for maintaining a proper respect for God.

But there are two responses I would like to share regarding this concern for respect.

First, remember when you were a young child. Did the title "daddy" ever imply disrespect? No, on the contrary. I have often overheard my children say, "That's my daddy!" with the greatest pride, respect, and love. Do I mind being called "Daddy"? Are you kidding? That, to me, is a badge of great honor.

Second, I am not suggesting that we call God "Daddy." I don't think in our language the word "Daddy" carries with it enough of an appropriate sense of awe and reverence for the all-powerful Creator, Judge, and Ruler of the universe. In this regard, perhaps it was wise that the biblical translators did not translate the word *Abba* directly to the word "Daddy," even though that would have represented a literal translation.

May I suggest that we add a new word to our vocabulary? The word, of course, is *Abba*. It combines the affection, confidence and closeness of "Daddy" with the appropriate and necessary sense of awe and reverence.

For this reason, you will not see the word "Daddy" directly applied to God in the rest of this book. When the word "daddy" appears, it will be applied to a human daddy and used as an illustration.

What God Is Like

Now, before diving in to immerse ourselves in the discovery of God's Abbahood and our childhood, we need some guidelines to follow in our study. It is not enough at all for us to say, "God is like your dad." Maybe your dad was a tyrant or maybe your dad abdicated his responsibility as dad altogether.

I had one patient who was a fine Christian woman but who couldn't refer to God as her Father. Why? Because of the horrible experiences which she had actually endured, inflicted on her by her earthly father. It took a lot of work before she could accept God's Fatherhood and Abbahood as a replacement for what she'd never had.

Another patient found that she got angry whenever she prayed. This was also due to her past experiences with her natural father. As a solution, she analyzed every sentence she prayed and decided whether her emotions were directed to her earthly father or to God. Surprisingly, more than three out of every four sentences she prayed were emotionally aimed at her earthly father and not at God.

Many wrong emotions and ideas that people have about God come from our tendency to project onto God the traits of our own earthly fathers.

If we were to use this projection method in our study, we could be in real trouble, because what some people think is good fathering makes others nauseous.

Rather than basing our study on human experience and false assumptions about God, we must base our study on the Bible and compare that to human experience. This method will protect us from attributing false ideas to God. It will also teach us about good parenting.

The Lord did not set His love on you nor choose you because you were more in number than any of the peoples, for you were the fewest of all peoples, but because the Lord loved you and kept the oath which He swore to your forefathers. . .

Deuteronomy 7:7–8

4
AFFECTIONATE ABBA

We can learn a lot about the relationship between two people by listening to their conversations. A loving, affectionate relationship produces loving, affectionate communication.

Recently, my wife and I put our two daughters on an airplane (with their uncle) to visit their grandparents. As we did that, the older daughter said in her special grown-up way, "I love you, Daddy, and I'll miss you." The little one said, "Daddy, I be going to miss you."

Tears of joy and love welled up inside me as I expressed my affection for them and accepted theirs for me. This open exchange of affection is one part of the "daddy" stage of parenting that I treasure.

A Kiss, a Hug, and a Tickle

Almost every day I receive a picture or a "prize" of some kind from both of my girls. With the prize often comes these words: "This is for you, Daddy, because I love you." As daddy, I can say, "I love you" just as easily to them. I'm never embarrassed to ask for kisses, give them, or get them.

Whenever I'm home at my daughters' bedtime, I pray with them and give them both a kiss, a hug, and a tickle. Some nights they ask for an extra tickle or two extra kisses. Happily, I accommodate them. I'm always glad to show my affection for them no matter how many kisses, hugs, and tickles I have to give.

But showing affection works two ways. If I walk in while they're playing and say, "Daddy needs a hug," I'm sure to get at least one—usually I get many more than that.

If I've expressed myself well enough so far, I imagine that most readers can get in touch with some emotion. For many, it may be a combination of joy, a little smiling, mixed in with perhaps a longing to be able to express their emotions so freely. I'm sure some readers could really use a hug today.

I can't think of any term more affectionate than the term "daddy." Daddies (as well as mommies) supply their children with the extra love they need in order to have those "warm fuzzy" feelings.

No Risk

In every other relationship, there is some risk involved in saying, "I love you." But for a daddy and his little child, neither usually worries about rejection by the other. Whether daddy or child, if we love, we can say so during the "daddy" stage.

When children grow older, they and their parents become less expressive of their affection. When did you last hear and see a teenage boy or girl squeal, "Daddy's home!" then run to greet him with a hug and a little treasure they'd made just for him?

I suppose this change is a natural part of the growing process. After children mature and become adults, they usually move away from their parents. But something is lost when children grow out of the magic of the "daddy" days. Those "daddy" days are special because of the affection which is freely exchanged without hesitation or embarrassment.

As believers, the progression of our relationship with God is not like that of our parent-child relationships. With God, we don't slide from open affection to a more reserved expression of love. On the contrary, God progressively reveals more of Himself in order to relate to us in a way that is constantly more affectionate and expressive.

A History of Love

The story of God's love begins with God making a

choice. God decided to love us. "The Lord did not set His love on you nor choose you because you were more in number than any of the peoples, for you were the fewest of all" peoples, but because the Lord loved you . . ." (Deut. 7:7–8).

God didn't just happen upon Adam and Eve in the Garden of Eden and discover Himself loving them accidentally. He first chose them. He decided to love them, and then created them to be objects of His love.

There is a profound truth in John 3:16 that may be often overlooked. The truth is that love is giving. "God so loved the world that He gave . . ." What did He give? We know that He gave His Son. But we are limited in comprehending the other gifts which He gave. How can a finite mind understand an infinite love?

It seems that God's love was first expressed in the gift of life, which He so freely bestows to us. The only reason we exist as living creatures is that (just like Adam and Eve) God wanted to love us. The rest of history is the story of God trying to convince mankind that He really means it when He says He loves us.

Through Scripture, we know Adam and Eve chose independence (wanting to be their own gods) rather than obedience to God the Father. But God even used man's disobedience as an opportunity to display His gracious love. "The Lord your God turned the curse into a blessing for you because the Lord your God loves you" (Deut. 23:5).

Down through history God has continued to draw His people to Himself. "I have loved you with an everlasting love; therefore I have drawn you with loving-kindness" (Jer. 31:3).

God has shown Himself to us through nature, through His Word, through His Son, and through His other adopted children. In response to all of that—praise the Lord—some people respond to His love. When they do, they say, "Because Thy loving-kindness is better than life, my lips will praise Thee" (Ps. 63:3). And they experience the joy of a new perspective. For the first time, they can accurately regard the universe and all of history as an affectionate Father's expression of love for His children.

Unconditional Love

God's love for us is not conditional. He loves us even when we do wrong. Paul wrote, "God demonstrates His own love towards us, in that while we were yet sinners, Christ died for us" (Rom. 5:8). To the Ephesians he wrote, "But God, being rich in mercy, because of His great love with which He loved us, even when we were dead in our transgressions, made us alive together with Christ (by grace you have been saved)" (Eph. 2:4–5).

The thrust here is that we were loved even

while we were sinners. Before we gave our lives to Christ, God loved us—and He doesn't stop loving us even if we disobey Him. Even an imperfect parent doesn't stop loving that easily, and certainly because God is Love (1 John 4:8), His love is better than human love.

Many people try to put conditions on God's love for them. This could be due to past experiences with parents who seemed to communicate a conditional love. But God's love is there for sure and we can rest in it as safely as Trisha did when she jumped out of the tree and said, "Catch me, Daddy!" She knew that under no conditions would her daddy willingly let her drop.

Most children actually believe that they are loved when they are good and not loved when they are bad. Some parents are foolish enough to actually say, "I don't love you when you do that." Other parents don't come right out and say it. But little ones find it pretty hard to feel loved when grown-ups two or three times their size yell at them or hit them.

After my daughters have been disciplined or spanked, it is not unusual for them to say, "Daddy, do you love me even when I'm naughty?" They need the security of knowing I am their father and no matter what, I will always love them.

While some parents may be more careful about showing unconditional love than others, it is fairly unusual for a parent to decide not to be a parent any longer. Even if a son or daughter is arrested for selling heroin to 10-year-olds, not many parents will disown him or her. The parents will, of course, be angry and greatly hurt. But we look down on parents who disown their children when they (the children) don't live up to their parents' expectations.

God's love for us is not dependent on our good behavior. To be in God's family, we must acknowledge our need, and believe on His Son. Then God makes us His children. He forgives and forgets every shortcoming we have ever had and ever will have.

Positionally, God sees all believers as being in Christ. To be in Christ means that to God we look perfect—not because of our good works, but because of Christ's work on our behalf.

Realistically, God knows that we aren't perfect yet—we still sin. When we sin, our fellowship with God is broken. But we don't have to pay for our sins or suffer God's wrath because of them— Jesus already paid the penalty. Because of Christ's work, we can be forgiven and restored to fellowship with God even after we sin.

I often tell my patients, "If you could suddenly make yourself perfect between now and 7 P.M., God wouldn't love you any more a month from now than He does right now. You are already 100 percent perfect in His sight."

God's affection for us is so consistent because it is not based on our behavior or on our emotions. God's love is based on His choice which is immutable or unchangeable.

So What?
What does God's unchanging love mean to me and to you? Remember that one characteristic of the "daddy" stage of parenting is the free, confident, and unselfconscious expression of affection.

If we are confident of God's absolutely unchangeable love, we should be able to freely communicate with Him. We don't have to be afraid of His wrath if we fall short of His standard. We don't have to hide or avoid Him. He already knows about us, and He loves us anyway.

He does not delight in the strength of the horse; He does not take pleasure in the legs of a man. The Lord favors those who fear Him, those who wait for His loving-kindness.
Psalm 147:10–11

5
HE DELIGHTS IN US

Recently, I saw a television commercial for instant movies. The advertising campaign had been cleverly centered on the pride parents feel as they watch their child's first steps. The advertising people know that most parents want to relive that delightful moment.

At a moment like a child's first steps, most parents experience a mixture of joy and pride. That brings to mind how often we've heard the phrase "my pride and joy" associated with one's child.

Where did we humans get the capacity for that combination of special feelings which we call "delight"? Who designed us? The answer to both questions is the same. God gave us the capacity to experience some of those same emotions that He feels toward us at times.

Love or Delight?

The easiest way to distinguish between delight and love is to recognize the two words "at times." Because delight includes a sense of pride, we realize that there are times when God is particularly proud of us and pleased with our attitude or behavior.

There are also other times when, even though God still loves us, He couldn't be delighted with our behavior or attitude. So, God's love is continual. Yet His delight in us is a unique mixture of joy and pride that comes at special times.

Someone is probably wondering what the Bible teaches about this. Perhaps the most straightforward biblical statement of God's delight is, "Blessed be the Lord your God who delighted in you." This identical phrase appears both in 1 Kings 10:9, and 2 Chronicles 9:8.

Psalm 37 also deals with this subject of the Lord's delight.

> The steps of a man are established by
> the Lord; and He delights in his way.
> When he falls, he shall not be hurled
> headlong; because the Lord is the One
> who holds his hand. I have been young,
> and now I am old; yet I have not seen the

righteous forsaken, or his descendants begging bread. All day long he is gracious and lends; and his descendants are a blessing (Ps. 37:23–26).

Here, the psalmist presents a picture which is consistent with the characteristics of Abba. God establishes the way He wants His children to live, and God delights when His children obey Him.

Notice verse 24. Even when we stumble, we don't tumble down the mountainside or drop off a cliff. Nor does God throw us far away from Himself. Rather, He holds our hands to prevent our headlong plunge into destruction.

Then the Psalmist David added a word from his personal experience. He said that in all of his life (and he was then old) he had never seen God forsake His children.

God is delighted when we walk right, and because He delights in us, He rescues us when we fall. "He also brought me forth into a broad place; He rescued me, because He delighted in me" (2 Sam. 22:20). A similar statement is found in Psalm 22. "Commit yourself to the Lord; let Him deliver him; let Him rescue him, because He delights in him" (Ps. 22:8).

Because He delights in us, God is always willing to rescue us when we fall. But we must allow Him to do it. As a teenager, I remember being greatly moved by the following analogy which a

speaker used to describe the way we often relate
to God:

As we travel on the ship of life, some of us
realize our need for the Saviour. We invite Him
on board and usually prepare a beautiful stateroom where we expect Him to stay. Then we go
back up to the bridge and take the helm once
more.

After a while, we may run into a storm or run
aground. Then we go and ask God if He'll rescue
us from the trouble we've gotten into. He invari-
ably does.

But tragically, we usually say, "Thanks a lot"
and take over the helm again. We expect Him to
return to His stateroom until the next crisis.

I like that analogy because it describes our
typical way of acting. While God is always ready to
rescue us when we ask, He is particularly delighted when we travel His way in the first place.

Conditions of Delight
As we survey the biblical use of the word *delight*,
we see very clearly that delight is conditional. The
psalmist shows us the contrast clearly. " [God]
does not delight in the strength of the horse; He
does not take pleasure in the legs of a man. The
Lord favors those who fear Him, those who wait
for His loving-kindness" (Ps. 147:10–11).

God is pleased when our focus of attention is
exclusively on Him. He doesn't want us to be

particularly pleased with the strength of our horses (or in our society, perhaps "horsepower" conveys more). God is not delighted when we focus on our own strength.

Religious ceremonies designed to impress God don't earn His favor either. " 'What are your multiplied sacrifices to Me?' says the Lord. 'I have had enough of burnt offerings of rams, and the fat of fed cattle. And I take no pleasure in the blood of bulls, lambs, or goats' " (Isa. 1:11).

A false ceremony is a lot like hanging a picture of Jesus on the bridge, but keeping Him in the stateroom. It is a hollow act. " 'Let him who boasts boast of this, that he understands and knows Me, that I am the Lord who exercises loving-kindness, justice, and righteousness on earth; for I delight in these things,' declares the Lord" (Jer. 9:24).

God's Word is so clear here. He wants our lives, our minds, our attitudes, and our activities to be focused on Him.

But what if you're in a secular line of work? How can that be God-centered? Is the work produced by a God-centered tool and die maker measurably different from that of his fellow worker? No, I think not. The work probably isn't much different, but the *worker* is.

I'm sure that God expects us to do our best in every endeavor. But even more than the quality of our product, He is concerned with the quality of our faith in Him. The better we know God, the more attention we give Him; the more our lives are filled up with viewing the world as He does, the more He is delighted.

Daddy Is Bigger Than Me

Abba is also pleased when we let Him be who He is. One reason why the "daddy" stage of parenting is more enjoyable than the later years is because of the way that small children relate to their fathers. There is likely to be much less of a power struggle between a daddy and his toddler than between that same daddy and his teenager.

When compared to a teenager, a young child is much more likely to accept the fact that his daddy is bigger, smarter, and more powerful. A little one is typically more pleased to be dependent on his father. He sees his father's strength as a source of security rather than as a threat to him. We need to see Abba the same way.

Divine Dependency

Of course as children grow up, it is perfectly natural for them to become gradually less dependent on their parents. In this aspect, a parent-child relationship is different than our relationship with God. We should never grow out of a position of secure dependency on our Abba.

God says that we must become like little children to be part of His kingdom. "Whoever then humbles himself as this child, he is the greatest in the kingdom of heaven" (Matt. 18:4). Being child-like means lacking power struggles; it means depending and trusting in God, and acknowledging our needs, our limitations. Here are three verses which support this.

"Not that we are adequate in ourselves to consider anything as coming from ourselves, but our adequacy is from God" (2 Cor. 3:5). Paul also wrote, "If any man among you thinks that he is wise in this age, let him become foolish that he may become wise" (1 Cor. 3:18). Jesus said, "Whoever exalts himself shall be humbled; and whoever humbles himself shall be exalted" (Matt. 23:12).

God deplores man's self-sufficiency. This is one concept that is extremely difficult for many modern evangelicals to accept and apply. Our culture rewards self-sufficiency, but for the child of God, independence is perhaps the greatest vice.

We cannot see God, but the more we act and feel toward Him like a young child feels about his daddy (having honor, respect, and confidence in Him, being dependent on Him, and secure because of Him), the more delighted Abba is with us.

Not long ago we moved to a new house. My second-grade daughter had to walk to school. She noticed a couple of older boys in the neighborhood, one of whom was a notorious bully, and for

awhile she was afraid to walk alone. Then, for
several days I walked along, first with her, then
perhaps 50 feet behind her. As you can imagine,
her attitude was totally different when she knew I
was watching her—just in case.

God is delighted when we acknowledge our
weaknesses and our needs and depend on Him as
a little child would depend on his daddy. We are
told that we must become as children.

Remember what it was like to be a young child?
Imagine yourself sitting on your daddy's lap.
There is a loud thunderstorm outside, but you are
safe because you are with your daddy. If it's been
a while since you felt that same warm, secure
feeling with God, both you and Abba will enjoy a
closer, warmer, more dependent relationship
that comes when there is no power struggle. Abba
delights in your trusting Him.

It is for discipline that you endure; God deals with you as with sons; for what son is there whom his father does not discipline? But if you are without discipline, of which all have become partakers, then you are illegitimate children and not sons.

Hebrews 12:7–8

6
DADDY'S DISCIPLINE

We come now to discuss one of the most important responsibilities of a father, and that is discipline. The word *discipline* comes from the same root as our word *disciple*. A disciple is a taught or trained one. Christ's disciples followed Him in order to be specially taught or trained by Him.

Discipline, then, means teaching, training, and correcting. The Bible uses "chastisement" interchangeably with the word *discipline*.

Discipline or Punishment?
Even though some people don't know it, there is a big difference between discipline and punishment. Specifically, punishment means paying the penalty for something you did wrong in the past.

You can visualize it as an arrow pointing backwards. Discipline, on the other hand, is focused on future growth, improvement, and correction. Visualize discipline as an arrow pointing forward.

So what? Well, Jesus paid the penalty for all our sins. He already took our punishment. There is only one punishment for sin and that is death. The wages of sin is death, but the free gift of God is eternal life through Jesus (Rom. 6:23).

The point is that our heavenly Father does not punish us. Jesus already suffered our punishment. God's love is unconditional. He loves us even when we're disobedient. True, He hates our sin. But Jesus paid that punishment. What is left is our own need to grow, to improve, to learn, to be taught how to be more Christlike. This very necessary training comes through God who disciplines (or chastens) us.

Anger

As a father, I usually respond to naughtiness in my children in two different ways. I suppose these two ways of responding are true for all parents. The first way is to respond in anger. If I have been personally disturbed by a child interrupting me or stepping on my toe or perhaps waking me from a nap, I might get angry. At this point my feelings are very self-centered. I'm thinking only of what's best for me—I want to get even.

This is when punishment is likely to be inflicted. But the excellent principle "Never discipline in anger" should be applied. We should never spank our children or use any physical force when we're angry. We are inflicting punishment, getting even, and being self-centered—and if we *are* angry, we're hitting a lot harder than we imagine.

A child is not equipped to bear the full weight of his parents' anger. When we respond in anger to our children, they feel rejected, unloved, frightened, and very insecure.

Imagine, or try to remember, how you felt when you were a small child. You were totally dependent on your parents for your survival. Physical and emotional needs were met by your parents—or they were not met. When the source of your survival (who was probably twice your size) raised his voice or hit you, you felt very alone.

This first type of parental response (anger and selfishness producing fear, rejection, and insecurity) is not the way that our heavenly Father responds to us. It is true of earthly parents sometimes, but it is not the response of God to His children.

Love

Sometimes I respond to my children in anger. But at other times when they misbehave, I respond in love. Compared with an angry reaction which is self-centered, a loving reaction is child-centered.

By responding in love, the parent shows that his thoughts are not on his own needs and feelings. Instead, his thoughts are focused on the needs and emotions of his child. This type of response is intended to help the child grow up to be a better person. This is discipline rather than punishment.

Proper discipline, even in the form of a spanking, does not produce fear in a child. It is not fun or pleasant for the parent or the child. But when it is done with love, it often brings the parent and the child closer. The child respects the parent and grows through the experience.

This second way of response—loving discipline—is how God responds to us when we are in need of improvement. As a result, we develop a sense of confidence and security—and we draw closer to God.

Love Me, Spank Me

Parents often remark that their children need limits and seem much happier for a while after they have been disciplined. This is true with my own children.

To children, proper discipline brings a sense of security. They know that their parents are keeping an eye on them. Children feel secure because they realize that they are not totally responsible for themselves. Somehow, children seem to understand that loving discipline shows that their parents really care about them.

God's response of loving discipline (chastisement), demonstrates His love. This is well documented in the Bible. "I will be his Father, and he shall be My son. If he commit iniquity, I will chasten [discipline] him with the rod of men, and with the stripes of the children of men; but My mercy shall not depart away from him" (2 Sam. 7:14–15, kjv).

Here God clearly says that He will discipline us (His children) when we need it. But this doesn't mean that He will leave us or withhold His mercy and love.

In the New Testament, we read:

> And you have forgotten the exhortation which is addressed to you as sons, "My son, do not regard lightly the discipline of the Lord, nor faint when you are reproved by Him; for those whom the Lord loves He disciplines, and He scourges every son whom He receives." It is for discipline that you endure; God deals with you as with sons; for what son is there whom his father does not discipline? But if you are without discipline, of which all have become partakers, then you are illegitimate children and not sons. Furthermore, we had earthly

fathers to discipline us, and we respected them; shall we not much rather be subject to the Father of spirits and live? For they disciplined us for a short time as seemed best to them, but He disciplines us for our good, that we may share His holiness. All discipline for the moment seems not to be joyful, but sorrowful; yet to those who have been trained by it, afterwards it yields the peaceful fruit of righteousness (Heb. 12:5–11).

The classic New Testament passage about the vine and the branches also deals with the matter of the believer's spiritual fruit. "Every branch in Me that does not bear fruit, He takes away; and every branch that bears fruit, He prunes it, that it may bear more fruit" (John 15:2). This means that we will be disciplined when we need to grow, and pruned even when we *do* bear fruit.

When I am aware of a problem situation occurring, my natural reaction is to ask, "Why me, God? I've been good." By reacting that way, I am assuming that I am being punished—but I'm not. Christ took all my punishment because I am an adopted son and a grafted branch.

Troubles are not a sign of punishment. Rather, they are a sign either of disciplining or pruning. Neither disciplining nor pruning is a negative reaction on God's part. In disciplining us, God proves His love. By pruning us, God acknowledges that we have been bearing fruit.

We should learn to stop reacting as if God is an angry, irrational, and unpredictable Parent who is just waiting for us to get out of line so He can belt us. "As many as I love, I rebuke and chasten; be zealous therefore, and repent" (Rev. 3:19, KJV).

God *is* a Parent Figure, but a loving One. Earthly parents are sometimes loving and sometimes selfish. But God is consistent. By getting to know Him better, we can consciously separate our concepts and emotions about Him that are appropriate from those which are not.

Appropriate Responses

Specific suggestions in this regard include several steps.

1. *Identify emotions and expectations that you have or have had about your parents*. Do this separately for mother and father. You may also need to include stepparents, grandparents, and others who may have had a significant part in your upbringing. Don't be afraid to write down the negative emotions. This list is just for your own reference.

2. *Identify emotions and expectations that you have or have had about God*. This will probably be much harder than the first step. Typically, people respond to this assignment by rambling

about theology, by ignoring their emotions, or by saying only positive things.

Let me give you an example of what I mean. When was the last time you prayed about something and got "No!" for an answer? Maybe you reacted by thinking, *I never get what I want,* or *It's not fair,* or *Promises, promises—only empty promises.* These are the kinds of emotions you need to identify.

3. *Once you have become aware of negative feelings or expectations about God, see if they are similar to feelings you have or have had about your parents.* If these emotions are not on your parent list, you may have overlooked the feelings in regard to your parents. Now that you are aware of them, see if they belong there on the parent list instead of with God.

4. *Train yourself to raise a little invisible red flag whenever a negative emotion or expectation arises regarding Abba.*

5. *Give yourself some correct input.* When you become aware of negative emotions that you feel toward God, remind yourself that God really is not like that. Ask God to help you forget those negative feelings that have been left over from another relationship.

6. *Get to know God better.* Knowing God includes studying carefully who He is and what He is like. The more effort you put into this, the more results you will see.

Be angry, and yet do not sin; do not let the sun go down on your anger.
Ephesians 4:26

7
ANGRY
WITH ABBA

In the previous chapter, we saw that God's discipline of His children is fair and it is administered with love and understanding. But there is a third factor involved in God's discipline. God's discipline can be rejected by us and therefore be in vain.

In the Book of Proverbs we read, "My son, do not reject the discipline of the Lord, or loathe His reproof, for whom the Lord loves He reproves, even as a father, the son in whom he delights" (Prov. 3:11–12). And in the Book of Jeremiah we read, "In vain have I struck your sons; they accepted no chastening" (Jer. 2:30).

Do you remember ever being disciplined as a youngster when you felt it wasn't fair? It has happened to most of us, whether it was the whole class being punished for one person's behavior or you being disciplined for something your brother did.

A Broken Relationship

Do you remember the feeling you had when you experienced unfair discipline? You probably felt as if a brick wall were being built between you and the unfair authority figure.

Many times we accuse God of being unfair. When we do, we are rejecting His discipline or His opportunity for our growth. Instead of openly communicating with Him, we are busy constructing a brick wall between ourselves and our Abba. We feel isolated and angry—and as a result, we don't grow.

Once when I was a young boy, I had been promised that when my father came home, he would spank me. When the appointed time came, I remember entering the room in complete control of my emotions. I was spanked as promised, but I did not cry or flinch or show pain in any way. I stood up, said, "Thank you" (not meaning it, of course), and walked out.

I refused to humble myself, refused to accept discipline. We often do the same thing to God. We become angry or accuse Him of being unfair. Sometimes even when we acknowledge His right to discipline us, we can—by refusing to accept His discipline—keep ourselves from spiritually grow-ing and benefiting from the experience.

When we refuse to humble ourselves and acknowledge our position as God's children, our relationship with Him suffers. It suffers in the same way that my relationship with my parents suffered because I rejected their discipline.

Stiff Necks
In the Book of Exodus, God often referred to the Israelites as being "stiff-necked." This word de-scribes my attitude that day as a boy. Sadly, it can also be applied to the attitudes of each of us at one time or another. To be stiff-necked means simply that we refuse to acknowledge someone else's control or authority over us.

As children of God, we may well say that we acknowledge God's authority. But I would have to be pretty foolish to think that the Creator of the universe does not also have sovereignty over me. He does.

But that is not the end of the struggle. For many Christians, it is only the beginning—be-cause unwilling dependency produces resent-ment.

Many of us have heard the story of the young boy who lost a power struggle with his dad. The father wanted his son to sit down. The child finally sat, but was heard to mutter, "I'm sitting on the outside, but I'm standing on the inside."

In our culture, it is not particularly unusual for grown children to borrow money from their parents, perhaps for a down payment on a house. The parents are often mystified when, shortly after coming to their children's rescue, the children suddenly become unresponsive, irritable, cold, and even resentful.

"What happened?" the parents often ask. "Did we do something wrong?" They may never discover the simple explanation: Unwilling dependency produces resentment.

"But they asked me for the money," the parents reply. No matter, it is still unwilling dependency because the children feel they have nowhere else to go for the money. So shortly after the loan transaction, the children often feel resentful. Unfortunately, the children rarely know why any more than the parents do.

What is the point of all of this? The point is that when we give in to God unwillingly, or observe some action that God initiates which upsets us, we get angry.

I Don't Like Your Plan

I am reminded of a young seminary student who came to me seeking relief from his depression. As we talked, it became evident that he had a great deal of anger. When he was questioned about it, he replied that he really felt angry with everything he could think of—trees, bushes, traffic lights, people, wallpaper—everything! (I've noticed that when people are angry with everything, they are often angry with the *Source* of everything, God.)

As our discussion continued, this seminary student finally admitted that some of his classmates were much smarter than he was. Some were better speakers, and some were more adequate leaders. He was not as gifted as some of the students—and he didn't like it. It made him angry.

Basically, his attitude could have been summed up like this: "God, I don't like what You've done with me and I don't like what You are doing. I don't like Your plan. I would like things to be my way rather than Your way."

Until that young man acknowledged that God knew best, he was unhappy. His relationship with God (as well as with himself and with others) was hindered by a brick wall of stubbornness.

By the way, I am not implying that *all* depression is a result of being angry with God. Most depression comes from not facing or feeling an unpleasant, but real emotion. That emotion can be grief, anger, disappointment, or hurt. But this student's depression was caused by his refusal to admit and feel his anger toward God.

Bad Results
Being angry with God will produce a lot of results, and all of them are bad. Anger with God usually

produces withdrawal from Him and therefore hurts our relationship with Him. This results in a self-centered or self-focused life, which is never as rewarding as a Spirit-controlled life.

Rebellion, or fighting against God, is another evidence of our anger with God. Rebellion gets us into all kinds of trouble. We do things we would normally not do, or we avoid doing what we should do because we feel rebellious.

Symbolic Rebellion

Before we become too smug about our lack of rebellion, let's remember that a lot of our rebellions may seem rather small, almost incidental.

We often clutch one small area which we know we need to change—such as the need for more regular Bible study. We may even know that we will be happier if we stop bickering with God over the issue. But by not giving God the victory, we can say symbolically, "God, I'm letting You run most things—but I'm still in charge in this one area."

Some time ago, I had one missionary for a patient who was very well disciplined in her spiritual walk. She told me one day how she resented having to constantly write letters to her financial supporters. In that one area, she was chronically late. As we talked, she realized that she was using this area as a symbolic way of telling God that she could still control her own life.

Who is hurt by our little power struggles with God—our little symbolic rebellions? We may think that we hurt only ourselves, but that is not true. We hurt ourselves mostly. But we also hurt the people nearest to us because our attitude toward God affects our relationships with everyone else.

Rebellion against God, whether large in scope or mostly symbolic, exposes an area of our lives that is not sanctified. This is usually where Satan does most of his damage. Remember that Satan is clever and can inflict massive damage from what appears to be a small wound.

Suggestions for Growth

To improve in this area, we should admit our anger—confess it openly to God. In fact, we should admit it while we are still reacting, while we are still angry.

Am I suggesting that we yell at God? Let me answer that this way. If our inner spirit is yelling at God already, the natural thing to do is to withdraw from Him (just as Adam and Eve did when they had sinned).

But that withdrawal is just what we need to avoid. When we are angry with God, if we can tell Him about it, then we are still communicating with Him. He knows about it anyway so we're not shocking Him, and believe me, He can take it. So the first step is to acknowledge to ourselves that the anger is there. The second step is to tell God about it.

The third step is by far the most difficult. We must humble ourselves. This means that we acknowledge that God's way is better, because He is perfect, loving, and good. We must stop fighting God and admit that we prefer His way over our own.

God's discipline must be humbly accepted. We must acknowledge our faults, our weaknesses, our needs. We must believe that God knows what He is doing. "Therefore, let those also who suffer according to the will of God entrust their souls to a faithful Creator in doing what is right" (1 Peter 4:19). We must learn to trust God.

Thou dost scrutinize my path and my lying down, and art intimately acquainted with all my ways. Even before there is a word on my tongue, behold, O Lord, Thou dost know it all. . . . Such knowledge is too wonderful for me; it is too high, I cannot attain to it.

Psalm 139:3–4, 6

8
ABBA
KNOWS BEST

The title of this chapter is taken from an old television series known as "Father Knows Best." That program depicted a wise father who gave timely, gentle, and understanding guidance to his family to help them through life's traumas.

We would like to imagine ourselves as being as kindly and wise as that father. We would like to believe that we know best. But even that television father (who was supposed to know best) needed a crew of script writers who created contrived episodes in which he could prove his "wisdom."

In reality, we are no better than that actor was at knowing best—even though we would like to think we are. Yet, one necessity for a loving parent-child relationship is that our children believe that we know, if not best, at least better than they do. Parents want their children's respect.

I know of an alcoholic who one day took his young son with him to the liquor store. He saw his son look at him as he got out of the car and he knew that the little boy believed, "My daddy knows best." The man turned around, got back in the car, and drove away—without his liquor. To him, maintaining his son's respect was more important than satiating his addiction to alcohol.

Respect is an important part of parenting. Parents usually try to keep their children's respect intact as long as they can.

Of course, we usually don't expect that kind of unquestioning respect from our teenagers (although it might be nice). We know that as children grow up, they realize that their parents are not "all-knowing." Teens do a lot of thinking for themselves; this is necessary in order for them to become independent adults.

Become As Children

In the Book of Matthew we read that we must come to God as little children (Matt. 18:3). This means that God wants us to believe that He knows best—all of the time.

Once, when Jesus' disciples were discussing who among them was the greatest, Jesus used a child as an example.

And He called a child to Himself and set him before them, and said, "Truly I say to you, unless you are converted and become like children, you shall not enter the kingdom of heaven. Whoever then humbles himself as this child, he is the greatest in the kingdom of heaven. And whoever receives one such child in my name receives Me; but whoever causes one of these little ones who believe in Me to stumble, it is better for him that a heavy millstone be hung around his neck, and that he be drowned in the depth of the sea" (Matt. 18:2–6).

A child is pure and naive, not cynical. Rather a child's believing is completely innocent. He accepts at face value whatever his daddy says. Note the strong words of warning to anyone who ridicules a child of God (v. 6).

Abba knows best because He knows everything. Not only that, but He knows how to make us the happiest we can be. And He knows which areas in our lives to touch which will cause us to glorify Him.

"Then why am I so unhappy?" you may ask. "Why are my finances such a mess? Why am I stuck in this crummy job? Or this crummy house? Why am I not rich?" The questions and complaints could run on and on. Our response in general is, "OK, prove it."

Theologically, we believe that God is omniscient. That means that He is all-knowing. We also believe that God is good, loving, and wise.

But few of us really live as if we are children of a loving Daddy who knows everything there is to know. We often ignore the fact that our heavenly Father has designed a plan to make us happy and fulfilled, to help us grow into His mature children. We forget that He has all situations and circumstances in complete control. We don't really act like Abba knows best.

Bible Review

Let's quickly review a few of the Bible verses which demonstrate that Abba knows best. The writer to the Hebrews tells us, "There is no creature hidden from His sight, but all things are open and laid bare to the eyes of Him with whom we have to do" (Heb. 4:13).

David, in the Book of Psalms, wrote:

> You have searched me and You know me: You know when I sit down and when I get up; You understand from far away what I think. You watch me when I travel and when I lie down and know intimately all my ways. Before there's a word on my tongue, Lord, You know all

about it. You besiege me from behind
and in front and lay Your hand on me.
. . . Your hand would lead me, and Your
right hand hold me. . . . The night
shines like the day, and darkness is like
light. You created my inner being and
wove me together in my mother's
womb. I thank You for how marvelously
and wonderfully I am made. . . . Before
a single one of my days took shape they
were all prepared and written in Your
scroll (Ps. 139:1–5; 10; 12–14; 16, BECK).

Ezekiel recorded these words from the Lord:
"For I know the things that come into your mind,
every one of them" (Ezek. 11:5, KJV).

Another verse that tells about God's omni-
science is found in the Book of Proverbs. "The
eyes of the Lord are in every place, beholding the
evil and the good" (Prov. 15:3, KJV).

The Prophet Isaiah wrote, "Who has directed
the spirit of the Lord, or being His counsel or has
taught Him? . . . and taught Him in the path of
judgment, and taught Him knowledge, and
showed to Him the way of understanding?" (Isa.
40:13-14, KJV)

Our Bible review concludes with a verse from
the New Testament. "For who has known the
mind of the Lord? Or who has been His coun-
selor?" (Rom. 11:34, KJV)

Resting or Demanding Proof?

In *The Knowledge of the Holy* (Harper and Row), A.W. Tozer reminds us that true faith is resting in who God *is*. We can contrast this "resting" with our questions and doubts that we have mentioned before. Our human nature tends to demand action. We want tangible proof.

But when we demand proof from God, we place ourselves in the role of independent agents who need to be bargained with individually. In essence, we put ourselves in a position of judging God. This is not an attitude of faith and it does not produce joy.

A position of faith is based on the fact of who God is. All of the other aspects of life are interpreted on this basis—that God really does know best. To truly believe that God, our perfect heavenly Father, is in charge gives us a sense of security that can't be matched in human relationships. We know that everything is going according to His plan and that nothing will surprise Abba. Living by faith, we experience peace, rest, joy, and confidence—as well as a closer relationship with God.

Unfortunately, most of us don't live by faith—at least not all of the time. But consider this: The bad news that you got last week, the frightening rumor you heard yesterday, and the real disappointment you suffered today, were all part of the plan of your Abba who knows best.

Personal Responses

Two personal responses are necessary if we intend to live as if we really believe that Abba knows best. The first response is one of humility. We must acknowledge our limitations and our need. We need to admit that we aren't equipped to run our own lives. We're not smart enough. We won't ever grow up to be God. But we can be His children.

The second response should be one of gratitude. When we admit that we can't handle the responsibilities of God, we can be truly thankful that Abba can. He loves us and He is in control.

As you start each day, why not thank Abba in advance for the plan He's prepared for you that day? Surely, you will be surprised by what happens. But remember that He has had this in mind all along. Only trust Him. Abba knows best.

Blessed be the Lord, because He has heard the voice of my supplication. The Lord is my strength and my shield; my heart trusts in Him, and I am helped; therefore my heart exults, and with my song I shall thank Him.

Psalm 28:6–7

9
FIX IT, DADDY

"Daddy, will you fix my dolly? The arm's broken." As the very proud daddy of two little girls, I am asked this question, or one very much like it, several times a week.

As a loving daddy, I enjoy fixing broken toys for my girls. Sometimes the fixing is easy. Other times I wonder, *How am I going to fix that?*

But I want to please my children. I want them to be happy. And I want them to keep coming to me, so I do my best to fix things for them. I'm sure most loving daddies feel the same way.

"Too Busy"
We probably all have had some contact with fathers who tell their children, "Not now, I'm

busy." After a while, the children give up going to their busy fathers.

Even though there are plenty of the "too busy" dads around, they are beginning to be frowned on in our society. Parents should learn to make time to fix the broken toys, bandage the broken skin, and care about their children's broken hearts. Parents who do are more likely to have happier children than those parents who are always "too busy."

God cares about our hurts and our broken personal treasures. He cares and doesn't mind fixing things for us. However, we sometimes feel like this when we come to pray: "God, I hate to bother You again. I know I was here yesterday with some things I needed You to fix, but I have this problem. . . ."

We may not actually put it into words, but sometimes we act as if God is very busy and we shouldn't bother Him unless it is extremely important. This may have been true of our dad or mom, but it surely is not true of God. He is limitless in the time, energy, concern, and love He will use to fix our hurts.

Not only is He able to fix our hurts, but Abba wants to. He is willing. Let's look at some examples of this from the Book of Psalms.

"I was crying to the Lord with my voice, and He answered me from His holy mountain. I lay down and slept; I awoke, for the Lord sustains me. I will not be afraid of ten thousands of people who have set themselves against me round about" (Ps. 3:4–6).

The psalmist was doing exactly what many of us have done in church services or with friends. He was giving his testimony about how God had blessed him and had answered his prayers. He had been crying out to God. Then God helped him. The psalmist felt such peace that he went to sleep—he knew that the Lord would take care of him. He was no longer afraid.

Often we read through a psalm so quickly that we miss the significance that the writer intended. But let's take time to review this passage from Psalm 3. The order of these verses points out something important.

The psalmist was in a desperate situation. He was surrounded by tens of thousands of his enemies. But notice what he did. He prayed, he believed, and then he slept.

When he woke up, he still felt the same calm from the night before—even though the enemy camp was still surrounding him (v. 6). The visible answer to his prayer had not come yet. But the psalmist had his eyes off the enemy and on the Lord.

Since he knew the One to whom he was praying, the psalmist knew that he would be safe. He relaxed and stopped worrying. (As a pyschologist, I often wish I could somehow bottle that ability to pray, believe, and fall asleep in peace. What an antidote for worry!)

Now let's look at another psalm that deals with this same idea, Psalm 5. "Give ear to my words, O Lord, consider my groaning. Heed the sound of my cry for help, my King and my God, for to Thee do I pray. . . . But let all who take refuge in Thee be glad, let them ever sing for joy; and mayest Thou shelter them, that those who love Thy name may exult in Thee. For it is Thou who dost bless the righteous man, O Lord, Thou dost surround him with favor as with a shield" (Ps. 5:1–2, 11–12).

This psalmist was groaning and crying to God for help. The psalmist's intense cry was, no doubt, produced by great pain. Following his anguished cry, he became subdued and began to pray. As he talked with the Lord, his pain subsided. This settling down of his emotions was followed by praise to the Lord and a call for others to join in.

Notice verse 12. "Thou dost surround him with favor as with a shield." This psalm began with a man who was groaning with anguish. He asked God for help, and finally praised God for surrounding him with favor.

Here are a few brief excerpts from other psalms:

> And those who know Thy name will put
> their trust in Thee; for Thou, O Lord,
> hast not forsaken those who seek Thee.

. . . For He who requires blood remembers them; He does not forget the cry of the afflicted (Ps. 9:10, 12).

As for me, I said in my alarm, "I am cut off from before Thine eyes"; nevertheless Thou didst hear the voice of my supplications when I cried to Thee (31:22).

He heals the brokenhearted, and binds up their wounds (147:3).

The theme in these verses is clear and consistent: "I cried and He heard; I called and He answered." Isn't this just what we would expect from God? We are reminded again that God is good.

A.W. Tozer wrote, "The whole outlook of mankind might be changed if we could all believe that we dwell under a friendly sky and that the God of heaven, though exalted in power and majesty, is eager to be friends with us" (*The Knowledge of the Holy*, Harper and Row, pp. 89–90).

Our heavenly, perfect Father—our Abba—wants to become intimately involved in our lives. His concern does not stem from vengeance; He doesn't want to make us fail or make us miserable. Abba loves us and He wants us to let Him make us happy.

Sacrifice

Most fathers don't enjoy changing the soiled diapers of their children. Most mothers probably wouldn't claim that as their favorite duty either.

In spite of this, mothers (usually) and fathers (sometimes) respond to this need of their children with love. They actually don't mind getting dirty in order to clean up their children's messes. In love, parents look at the needs of their children rather than at their own comfort or convenience.

If a parent is loving toward a child, then that parent isn't self-centered. The parent is child-centered. This is the only way a parent can regularly change a child's messy pants and not mind— by caring about his child more than he cares about himself.

While struggling to make financial ends meet, most parents have had to sacrifice something in order for their children to get new shoes or go to the doctor. Parents rarely complain about this. It's part of being a parent to sacrifice for the children in order to meet their needs or help them in some way.

God is like that too, only much more so. Our biggest need is our sinful condition. Because the punishment for sin is death, our hope for eternal life is shattered. Our relationship with God is broken.

But Abba sacrificed His Son to save us. He did it for the same reason that we make sacrifices for our children. Because He loved us. He focused on our need more than on Himself.

This concept shows God's love to me in a new way. God was so love-focused on my need and so intent on saving me that He gave up His only Son. *That* is exciting!

Abba is waiting for you to come to Him with your messes and your hurts and to depend on Him. Tell Him all about your problems and ask Him for His help. He hears and He cares.

And all these, having gained approval through their faith, did not receive what was promised, because God had provided something better for us, so that apart from us they should not be made perfect.

Hebrews 11:39–40

10
CAN I HAVE THAT, DADDY?

Breathes there a parent in this country who has never heard those famous words, *Can I have that, Daddy?*

You don't even need to be in a toy store or a candy store. You can be in the frozen food section of the supermarket, or in the back of a paint store, or even in a hardware store. It can happen anywhere, at any time.

Where do children get such a trait? Well, maybe they've been listening to their parents pray. We do seem to ask God for a lot.

But God, like a good parent, wants us to be happy. He listens to our requests and, when it is appropriate for us, He gladly provides that for which we are asking—or something better. Does this mean we should test God by asking Him for anything we want?

Ask Anything

Our key verse is found in the Gospel of Matthew. "If you then, being evil, know how to give good gifts to your children, how much more shall your Father who is in heaven give what is good to those who ask Him!" (Matt. 7:11)

Just prior to this verse we read, "Ask, and it shall be given to you; seek, and you shall find; knock, and it shall be opened to you" (v. 7).

Matthew must have been impressed by God's promise of answered prayer. He also recorded these famous words of Jesus: "Truly I say to you, if you have faith as a mustard seed, you shall say to this mountain, 'Move from here to there,' and it shall move; and nothing shall be impossible to you" (17:20b).

Other Gospel writers conveyed this same idea. In the Gospel of Mark Jesus said, "Therefore I say to you, all things for which you pray and ask, believe that you have received them, and they shall be granted you" (Mark 11:24).

This is good news—prayer works! These "ask anything" verses remind me of the following saying: "Whatever you desire, and can clearly visualize, sincerely believe, and enthusiastically pursue will inevitably come to pass."

Sounds great, doesn't it? It makes us want to

strive for the impossible. There's only one problem. It doesn't work.

It Doesn't Work?

I can imagine what you're thinking. *Foster, have you gone crazy? Do you mean that prayer doesn't work?*

I'm not saying that prayer doesn't work. But I am saying that "God answers prayer" is *not* equivalent to "Anything you want, pursue, and believe in will take place." Very often we tend to confuse the two. It is possible for us to be sincerely wrong. Believing something does *not* make it so.

The "positive thinking" approach to prayer produces a lot of disillusioned believers. Recently, I heard about a pastor who believed God would provide the additional funds needed for a new church building.

Because of that belief, the church board set up a closing date at the bank. The pastor went to the bank on the appointed day with only part of the required money. He genuinely expected the rest of the money to be miraculously provided. It wasn't.

The bankers were not impressed with that kind of business management. The board of that church apparently felt that *believing* would bring in the lacking money. But God's plan was different from what the board believed.

Now why should we dwell on a negative story like that? Because we need to teach the whole Bible—not just the parts we like, and not just the parts that fit into our "give me" version of Christianity.

By Faith

The classic faith chapter, Hebrews 11, gives an accurate picture. "By faith Noah, being warned by God about things not yet seen, in reverence prepared an ark" (v. 7). "By faith Abraham, when he was called, obeyed" (v. 8). "By faith even Sarah herself received the ability to conceive, even beyond the proper time of life" (v. 11). But "all these died in faith, without receiving the promises" (v. 13). They saw the promises only from a distance.

Then we read that by faith Moses and the Israelites "passed through the Red Sea as though they were passing through dry land" (v. 29). "By faith the walls of Jericho fell down, after they had been encircled for seven days" (v. 30). And there were many others "who by faith conquered kingdoms, performed acts of righteousness, obtained promises, shut the mouths of lions, quenched the power of fire, escaped the edge of the sword . . . put foreign armies to flight. . . . Women received back their dead by resurrection. . ." (vv. 33–35).

Many people stop reading right there. When that happens, they get what I call the "Candyland" version of Christianity. It is totally positive and incomplete. It ignores the hardships that often come from living the life of faith.

But Hebrews 11 doesn't end there. The writer goes on to tell us that by faith "others were tortured . . . and others experienced mockings and scourgings, yes, also chains and imprisonment. They were stoned, they were sawn in two, they were tempted, they were put to death with the sword. . . . And all these, having gained approval through their faith, did not receive . . . because God had provided something better . . ." (v. 35–37, 39–40).

If the "Candyland" version of Christianity were true, then God would reward our ability to convince ourselves of something. We could have anything we want.

But the verses in Hebrews 11 refer to faith. Faith means that we depend on God as our Source. It is not the same as believing God will give us whatever we want.

The Real Picture

We now have two pictures of God. One shows a loving Father who answers prayer and knows best. The other depicts a "Candyland" version of a Father who gives us everything. The two pictures are clearly in conflict.

Finding the true picture is not difficult. Our heavenly Father is our Abba, but He's not our "sugar daddy." A parent who gives a child whatever the child wants doesn't love him, because the child does not know what is best for himself. Mostly, the child only knows that he wants *what* he wants, *when* he wants it.

Most of us realize that if we give a child whatever he demands, we end up with a spoiled brat. Later on, the brat becomes an ineffectual adult who has almost no ability to cope with society's demands. The spoiled child becomes an adult failure.

But when we acknowledge that Abba knows best, our outlook on life changes. When we want *His* plan more than anything else, He will give us what we want, according to His plan for us.

Well then, does God answer prayer or doesn't He? Certainly He does. But any parent knows that sometimes we need to tell our children "No" for their own good.

In the same way, God sometimes tells us "No" for our own good. Ultimately, "our own good" is best defined by God's plan for us. God wants His best for us, and He knows what will truly satisfy us.

Then, what happens when we ask, "Abba, can I have that?" God's answer is always consistent with His plan for us and with His perfect timing. His answer is determined by what is best for us. And, of course, He may give us something better than what we expected.

When I go shopping with my daughters and they ask for something, I check myself: *Is it an appropriate or good thing for them to have? Is it a good time for them to have it?* And, of course, *Can I afford it?*

God doesn't worry about affording our requests. But He must face the other two issues when we ask Him for something. His answers are based on His love and concern for us—and on His perfect plan.

Clothe yourselves with humility toward one another, for God is opposed to the proud, but gives grace to the humble.

1 Peter 5:5

11
PLEASE GOD, I'D RATHER DO IT MYSELF

Many of you probably remember the television commercials from a few years ago which were built around the phrase, "Please, Mother, I'd rather do it myself." The commercials were well-received because they picked up on a central theme of American life—independence.

Over 85 percent of all stress that occurs between parents and their children, even when those children are adults, comes from the issue of independence. It is both human nature and American culture to want to do whatever you please.

Probably every reader has heard of some college student who is working his way through college. We are all proud of a young person like that.

But the spiritual implications of our independent mind set are overwhelming. They spell material success and satisfaction, but spiritual failure and frustration.

When Satan rebelled against God, his sin was different in quality than the way we usually sin against God. Satan's attitude was, "You can't be God and rule the universe. *I* want to rule the universe instead." That was Satan's basic sin—active rebellion.

Man's most basic sin is different from Satan's. Most of us are content to let God be God of the universe. But we really don't care if He is God of the universe—as long as He doesn't bother us. Our basic sin, as opposed to active rebellion, is passive rebellion or simply ignoring God.

We tell God something like this: "You be God, rule the universe, take care of the stars and the planets. Meanwhile, I'm going to live my own life and ignore You as much as possible."

When I get into spiritual trouble, it is usually in this area. It may be because I started something on my own without seeking God's guidance. Or, maybe I started a project depending on God—but then when things went smoothly, I forgot God and depended on myself.

God's Principles
In God's Word, we discover that His goals for us are very different from the "independent and self-

reliant" standards of our society. God hates arrogant self-sufficiency.

In Deuteronomy we read, "You may say in your heart, 'My power and the strength of my hand made me this wealth.' But you shall remember the Lord your God, for it is He who is giving you power to make wealth, that He may confirm His covenant which He swore to your fathers, as it is this day" (Deut. 8:17–18).

The psalmist wrote, "Lo, this is the man that made not God his strength; but trusted in the abundance of his riches, and strengthened himself in his wickedness" (Ps. 52:7, KJV).

Let's look at a New Testament passage that discusses our dependence on God. It is found in John 15:1–9. This is the classic passage about the vine and the branches. It makes a very clear and powerful statement about dependence. Our strength comes only from the Lord. If we break away from that Source of strength, we dry up and wither.

God gave us another illustration which pictures our relationship with Him. It is the analogy of the potter and the clay. There are several verses from the Old and New Testaments that refer to this illustration.

In the Old Testament we read these words of Job: "I also am formed out of the clay" (Job 33:6, KJV). The Prophet Isaiah wrote, "Shall the potter be considered as equal with the clay? . . . Will the

clay say to the potter, 'What are you doing?' . . .
We are the clay, and Thou our Potter" (Isa. 29:16;
45:9; 64:8). "As the clay is in the potter's hand, so
are you in Mine hand" (Jer. 18:6, KJV).

In the New Testament, Paul wrote to the Romans, "Does not the potter have a right over the
clay, to make from the same lump one vessel for
honorable use, and another for common use?"
(Rom. 9:21)

Is the clay dependent on the potter? Yes. How
much so? Completely. What good is the clay without the potter? Absolutely none; it is soggy dirt.
Without the Potter we are useless.

Both of these images illustrate the same condition. It is a condition of dependency which is
essential to healthy spirituality. But it clearly
opposes society's standard of independence.

Doubtless or Dependent?
Previously, we were reminded that God anwers
the prayer of faith (refer to chapter 10). This does
not mean that God is obligated to answer our
prayers just because we can convince ourselves of
something. God does not necessarily answer the
psyched-up "I'm positive it's going to happen"
type of prayer.

We often have a mistaken idea of what it means
to pray in faith. The prayer of faith is a prayer
which is dependent on the Father. This concept of
prayer removes the problem that the "doubtless

prayer interpretation" brings. That problem, as we studied previously, is that sometimes "doubtless" prayers don't get the answers we were doubtless would take place.

God doesn't require perfect faith. He asks us to acknowledge that He knows what He is doing and that we are dependent on Him.

When we become aware of a problem or a need or a struggle in our lives, we should be alert to our tendency toward independence from God. Our desire for independence conflicts with our need for dependency on God. Independence makes us spiritually discontent. To curb our tendency toward independence, we must consciously cultivate a childlike attitude toward the Father.

We should never become so proud that we think we can serve God in our own strength. We can't live like Christ on our own. It is only through God's grace and strength that we can glorify Him.

In my counseling, I usually begin each session with a silent prayer. I acknowledge my weakness and my dependency on the Father and ask for His leading and His insights.

Yet even though I regularly do this, sometimes (especially after a couple of good sessions) I forget about God and strike out on my own. I tell God, "It's all right, Father. I can handle this one. You take a break." Of course, those are the sessions that fall flat.

Make no mistake about it, depending on God is

often difficult. We must consciously make an effort to depend on our Abba day after day. It takes a conscious effort from us because we naturally want to rely on ourselves. But by depending on God and living for Him, we can find spiritual satisfaction.

We must develop the habit of continually and consciously admitting to God, "Abba, I'd rather *not* do it myself." This is easy to say, easy to write, and hard to do. But our Father is delighted when we do rely on Him.

For I am convinced that neither death, nor life, nor angels, nor principalities, nor things present, nor things to come, nor powers, nor height, nor depth, nor any other created thing, shall be able to separate us from the love of God, which is in Christ Jesus our Lord.
Romans 8:38–39

12
THAT'S MY ABBA

In previous chapters we have seen that God wants us to view Him as our Father and even as our Abba. He loves us, He delights in us, He knows everything, and He has a plan for us.

With limitless love and patience, He disciplines us. He wants to fix our hurts and answer our prayers—because He is the good and perfect Abba.

All of these aspects of our Abba can make us proud of Him and can make us want to be close to Him. Most of us probably felt when we were younger that our daddy was the greatest one in the whole world. As we grew up, maybe we realized that he wasn't the absolute greatest after all. We probably still loved him anyway. But the more we got to know him, the more flaws we came to see.

The better we get to know our Abba, the more we realize that He really *is* the best Father of all. He doesn't just meet the standards for good parenting. He *sets* the standards for good parenting.

Love, compassion, discipline, and the ability to form a close relationship all got their beginnings from our very own Abba. When we have a close and deep relationship with Him, we can enjoy Him more—and we can enjoy all of life more. How do we cultivate a closer relationship with God?

In looking for biblical models, my mind went first to the close relationship between David and Jonathan depicted in the Old Testament.

David and Jonathan
We first read about the relationship between David and Jonathan after David had killed Goliath.

> Now it came about when [David] had finished speaking to Saul, that the soul of Jonathan was knit to the soul of David, and Jonathan loved him as himself. And Saul took him that day and did not let him return to his father's house. Then Jonathan made a covenant with

David because he loved him as himself. And Jonathan stripped himself of the robe that was on him and gave it to David, with his armor, including his sword and his bow and his belt (1 Sam. 18:1–4).

What can we learn here about close relationships? First, we see that "the soul of Jonathan was knit to the soul of David." That is not only a beautiful way to describe a close human relationship, but it also has obvious parallels for us as we develop a closer relationship with Abba.

Knitting two things together produces such a blending or fusion that we can no longer tell where one part ends and the other begins. If we want a close relationship with Abba, we first need to be sure we have been joined together with Him. He welcomes all who ask to be made part of His family through His Son's atoning work.

Next, we notice that Jonathan loved David as himself. Close relationships don't just happen. When we give only restricted parts of ourselves to others and keep the other parts off limits, our relationships become stifled. The more of ourselves we give to Abba, the closer we grow to Him. I've heard people say, "God can have this part of my life, but these other parts are still mine." These limited givers are also limiting the depths of their relationships with God.

Move In

In verse 2, we see that David moved in and lived with Jonathan's family. David and Jonathan spent time together. When two people are getting to know each other, the more time they invest in their relationship, the closer they will become.

How can we apply this to our relationship with Abba? By including Him in all of our activities during the day. Communication affects the quality of our relationships. When two people communicate only once a week, their relationship is not as strong as the relationship of two people who communicate all the time.

As David and Jonathan spent more and more time together, their relationship grew. The same thing can happen to our relationship with God. We need to get into the habit of becoming aware of Abba's presence with us all day long. We can do this by talking to Him throughout the day, and by reading His Word whenever we can. As we spend time with Him, we will naturally grow closer to Him.

"Then Jonathan made a covenant with David because he loved him as himself " (v. 3). Another word for *covenant* is *commitment*. A commitment to Abba might sound something like this: "Abba, I want to have a closer relationship with You. I want to spend more time with You. I want to put some regular effort into getting to know You better so we can be closer."

"Take My Coat, Please"

In verse 4 we read that Jonathan stripped himself. He gave his robe, his armor, his sword, his bow, and his belt to David. How shall we apply this to a growing relationship with Abba?

Stripping is humbling. We leave ourselves open to criticism by not hiding anything. This figurative (not literal) stripping is absolutely necessary in order to have a close relationship with someone. We can't get close to others if we're still wearing our armor.

Jonathan gave away his armor, his sword, and his bow to become vulnerable to his friend. In those days the belt was used to tie up the flowing garment and give freedom for running or fighting. Jonathan gave his belt away too. He limited his own freedom by his close association with David.

This is what happens in a close relationship. Some limits are applied to our freedom. Yet, at the same time, there are greater freedoms that we can take with our close companion.

Recently, I was teaching a class about relating to God as our Abba. As I taught, I held one of my daughters to illustrate certain aspects of the parent-child relationship. While I was talking, my daughter grabbed my tie and pulled it out of my vest.

At that point, one of the class members commented that a close relationship *does* permit greater freedom. No one else in the class that day would have considered pulling my tie, but my daughter knew that it would be all right.

In the same way, as we grow closer to God, we are allowed to exercise more freedom. The writer of the Book of Hebrews tells us that we should approach God boldly in prayer (Heb. 4:16). That kind of boldness comes only from a close relationship with the King.

In this passage, there is another matter we should notice. The robe and the armor which Jonathan gave to David had been marked and colored in such a way that people would identify the wearer as Jonathan, the king's son. At this time in their relationship, they were publicly identified as close friends.

A close relationship with Abba will also require us to publicly identify ourselves as being united with Him. That is what the word *baptism* means—identification. But there is more to identification or baptism than getting wet. Baptism is the official act which symbolizes that we are no longer hiding our relationship with Abba.

A Renewed Covenant

Later on in the relationship between Jonathan and David, we read these words: "Thus [Jonathan] said to [David], 'Do not be afraid, because the hand of Saul my father shall not find you, and you will be king over Israel and I will be next to you; and Saul my father knows that also.'

So the two of them made a covenant before the Lord" (1 Sam. 23:17–18).

Don't forget that according to usual custom, Jonathan was the rightful heir to his father's throne. But Jonathan said that the throne would be David's. He was willing to make a great personal sacrifice for his friend. In a close relationship, we often make sacrifices which we probably wouldn't make if we weren't involved so closely with another person.

In a growing relationship with God, we must relinquish ownership of ourselves. When we acknowledge that Abba is in charge, He will take over in our lives. Our motto will no longer be "I did it my way." Instead, we will declare, "To God be the glory."